Activities and Study Guide

Principles of Business

NINTH EDITION

Les R. Dlabay

James L. Burrow

Brad A. Kleindl

SOUTH-WESTERN
CENGAGE Learning

Australia • Brazil • Mexico • Singapore • United Kingdom • United States

SOUTH-WESTERN
CENGAGE Learning

For product information and technology assistance, contact us at **Cengage Learning Academic Resource Center, 1-800-423-0563**.

For permission to use material from this text or product, submit all requests online at **www.cengage.com/permissions**. Further permissions questions can be emailed to **permissionrequest@cengage.com**.

ISBN: 978-1-305-65304-7

Cengage Learning
20 Channel Center Street
Boston, MA 02210
USA

Cengage Learning is a leading provider of customized learning solutions with employees residing in nearly 40 different countries and sales in more than 125 countries around the world. Find your local representative at **www.cengage.com**.

Cengage Learning products are represented in Canada by Nelson Education, Ltd.

For your course and learning solutions, visit **ngl.cengage.com**.

Visit our company website at **www.cengage.com**.

Printed in the United States of America
Print Number: 01   Print Year: 2016

Activities and Study Guide

CONTENTS

Chapter 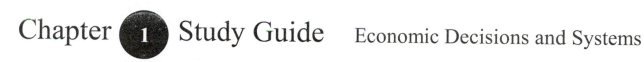 1 Study Guide   Economic Decisions and Systems

Part 1   True or False

Directions   Place a *T* for True or an *F* for False in the Answers column to show whether each of the following statements is true or false.

Answers

1. A video game is an example of a product that fulfills a need.

   1. _____

2. Tangible products you can purchase to meet your wants and needs are called goods.

   2. _____

3. When you decide to buy a jacket instead of a concert ticket, you are making a trade-off.

   3. _____

4. Capitalism is another name for a traditional economic system.

   4. _____

5. Competition forces businesses to search for new ways to satisfy customers' wants and needs.

   5. _____

6. The market price for a product is the point where demand exceeds supply.

   6. _____

7. Economists predict future changes in the economy.

   7. _____

8. China is the largest producer of goods and services in the world.

   8. _____

Part 2   Multiple Choice

Directions   In the Answers column, write the letter that represents the word, or group of words, that correctly completes the statement.

Answers

9. The basic economic problem is (a) having unlimited wants and needs but limited economic resources (b) deciding what goods and services to produce (c) identifying the goods and services available to you (d) determining how to satisfy needs and wants.

   9. _____

10. An important principle of the U.S. economic system is (a) the right to private property (b) the freedom of choice (c) competition (d) all of the above.

    10. _____

11. If freezing weather damages orange crops in Florida (a) the demand for oranges will decrease (b) the price of oranges will increase (c) the supply of oranges will remain unchanged (d) the price of orange juice will decrease.

    11. _____

12. Water, air, and minerals are examples of (a) consumer resources (b) natural resources (c) capital resources (d) human resources.

    12. _____

13. If you decide to purchase a digital copy of your favorite movie instead of a pair of jeans, the value of the jeans is the (a) market price (b) profit (c) opportunity cost (d) trade-off price

    13. _____

Part 3   Matching

Directions   In the Answers column indicate which economic system is best described by each statement.

   A.   command economy   C.   traditional economy
   B.   market economy   D.   mixed economy

Answers

14. Resources are owned and controlled by the people of the country.

    14. _____

15. The government decides what and how goods are produced.

    15. _____

16. Workers often use hand tools and readily available natural resources.

    16. _____

17. As countries become more developed, they often adopt this economic system.

    17. _____

18. Consumers base their decisions on their own self-interest.

    18. _____

Part 4   Activities

19. Review your own recent purchases and observe Internet ads or store signs that feature price changes. In the following table, list five examples of products or services for which you have noticed price changes. Identify the product or service; show whether the price change was an increase or decrease; and identify the reason for the price change.

Product or Service	Price Increase or Decrease?	Reason for Price Change
_____	_____	_____
_____	_____	_____
_____	_____	_____
_____	_____	_____
_____	_____	_____

20. The graph below represents the supply and demand for hammers. Using the data provided in this graph, write a paragraph discussing the relationship between supply and demand. Why is it important for businesses to have this type of information when producing or selling a product? Based on the information provided, what is the market price for a hammer?

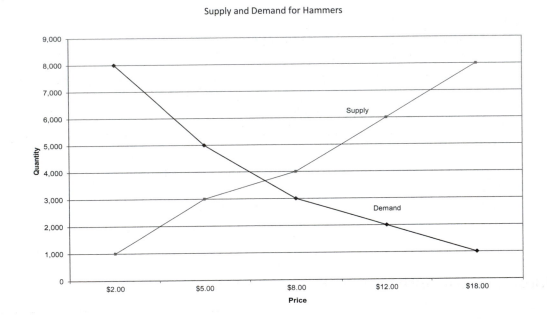

Supply and Demand for Hammers

Activities and Study Guide – Student Edition

21. For the past three years, Marci and Jeff have operated a small bake shop in their suburban neighborhood. Through their hard work and positive word-of-mouth advertising, the business has grown. Now Marci and Jeff are exploring ways to expand the business. They like their current location and have built a loyal customer base there, so they do not want to relocate. Because it is not possible to enlarge their current bake shop, they have considered opening a second location in another part of town. This would give their business exposure to new customers, but it also would require them to lease space, purchase ovens and other equipment, and hire and train new employees. Also, one of them probably would have to move to the new location to oversee operations. Another option is for Marci and Jeff to sell their baked goods to other businesses in town, such as restaurants and small grocery stores, for resale to their customers. That option would allow both Marci and Jeff to remain in their current location, but it would require them to upgrade their current ovens and add employees to handle the increased production. They also would need to hire a salesperson to contact local companies, purchase a delivery vehicle, and hire a driver to deliver the baked goods to locations around town. Use the steps in the decision-making process to help Marci and Jeff decide which option to pursue.

What is the problem Marci and Jeff face?

_____

_____

_____

What are the choices that Marci and Jeff must consider?

_____

_____

_____

_____

What are the advantages and disadvantages of each choice?

_____

_____

_____

_____

Which choice do you think is best for Marci and Jeff and why?

_____

_____

_____

_____

What should Marci and Jeff do once they have decided how they will expand their business?

_____

_____

_____

[This page left intentionally blank]

Chapter  2 Study Guide   Economic Activity

Part 1   Unscramble

Directions   Unscramble the following vocabulary words that were discussed in Chapter 2.

Answers

1. rutviiopdcyt   1. _____

2. ctsko   2. _____

3. yitqeu   3. _____

4. orseisnec   4. _____

5. ladfetnoi   5. _____

6. ertinsetetar (2 words)   6. _____

7. spytopirer   7. _____

8. prixcedine (2 words)   8. _____

9. lftiinano   9. _____

10. fdegtubitedci (2 words)   10. _____

11. vycrereo   11. _____

12. nycbeusciless (2 words)   12. _____

Part 2   Matching

Directions   In the Answers column, write the word or phrase from Part 1 above that correctly matches each statement below.

Answers

13. A period in which most people who want to work have a job, wages are good, businesses are producing a record number of goods, and the rate of gross domestic product (GDP) growth is increasing   13. _____

14. Can be increased by an improvement in management techniques   14. _____

15. Although there is a decrease in prices, people have less money to buy products   15. _____

16. A situation where a government spends more money than it takes in over a period of time   16. _____

17. A period in which unemployment begins to rise, demand begins to decrease, and businesses lower production   17. _____

18. An increase in prices and a decrease in the buying power of the dollar   18. _____

19. Represents the cost of money   19. _____

20. A phase represented by an increase in employment, demand for goods, and the GDP   20. _____

21. Movement of the economy from one condition to another   21. _____

22. Represents ownership in a corporation   22. _____

Part 3   Name That Measure

Directions   In the Answers column match the following economic measures with their descriptions.

  A.   gross domestic product (GDP)   C.   Consumer Price Index (CPI)

  B.   unemployment rate   D.   retail sales   **Answers**

23.   Compares the prices of a group of selected items each year to some earlier year   23._____

24.   The total dollar value of all final goods and services produced each year in a country   24._____

25.   Monthly measure of the sales of durable and nondurable goods bought by consumers   25._____

26.   The most widely used measure of national output   26._____

27.   The percentage of people in the labor force who are willing to work, are looking for work, but   27._____
are unable to find work

Part 4   Activities

28.   Business journals and newspapers regularly publish articles analyzing data that has been compiled by the government to examine the relative health of the economy. Conduct research to locate a current article dealing with one of the leading economic indicators, such as gross domestic product, consumer spending, interest rates, common stock prices, or unemployment rates. Read the article and write a report that addresses the issues listed below. Attach a copy of the article to your report.

    The cover sheet should include:

        Title of the article

        Source

        Date

        Your name

        Class

    The body of the report should present:

        A summary of the article.

        Discussion of how this information will affect you, your family, and your community.

        Discussion of how this information will affect local businesses, their employees, and the economy
in general.

    The conclusion of the report should present:

        Your opinion of the impact this information will have on the economy in the future.

        Your thoughts on the value of the information in the article.

Name _____ Class _____ Date _____

29. Employment statistics can relate valuable information about the economy. In times of prosperity, employment usually increases. However, in some industries, jobs may decrease even in times of prosperity if the production of goods to satisfy needs and wants is changing. A recent *Statistical Abstract of the United States* contains the following employment data for sectors of the U.S. economy for a four-year span.

INDUSTRY	EMPLOYMENT (in millions)		Calculation	PERCENTAGE OF CHANGE	RANK IN NO. OF JOBS
	Year 1	Year 4			
Wholesale/Retail	20.0	20.7	_____	_____	_____
Finance/Real Estate	9.4	9.7	_____	_____	_____
Transportation and Utilities	7.4	7.0	_____	_____	_____
Construction	9.9	10.1	_____	_____	_____
Manufacturing	19.6	16.9	_____	_____	_____
Education and Health Services	26.2	28.3	_____	_____	_____
Professional, Business and other Services	20.1	20.7	_____	_____	_____

1. Calculate the percentage of change in each of the categories and record it in the table. Round off your answers to the nearest percent.

   _____

2. Was there a decrease in employment in any category? If so, which one(s)?

   _____

3. Rank the categories based on the total number of people employed in each industry in year 4. Which category employed the most people?

   _____

4. Which category experienced the greatest percentage of increase? How many people does that percentage of increase represent?

   _____

5. What conclusions about the U.S. economy can you draw from this table?

   _____

[This page left intentionally blank]

Chapter ③ Study Guide Business in the Global Economy

Part 1 Yes or No

Directions Indicate your answer to each of the following questions by placing a check mark on the line under *yes* or *no* at the right.

Yes   **No**

1. Is foreign debt the amount of money that other countries owe the United States?   _____ _____

2. If a country imports more than it exports, does it have a trade deficit?   _____ _____

3. Does supply and demand affect the exchange rate?   _____ _____

4. Does a country's infrastructure refer to its climate and natural resources?   _____ _____

5. Are tariffs on certain goods used to restrict free trade?   _____ _____

6. Is the North American Free Trade Agreement (NAFTA) an agreement created by the United States, Mexico, and Japan?   _____ _____

7. Does licensing have a low financial investment and a high potential financial return?   _____ _____

8. Are franchise agreements popular with fast-food companies such as McDonald's, Wendy's, and Burger King?   _____ _____

Part 2 Completion

Directions In the Answers column, write the word or words needed to complete each sentence.

Answers

9. The primary effects on a country's level of economic development are its literacy level, agricultural dependency, and (?).   9. _____

10. Making, buying, and selling goods and services within a country is referred to as (?).   10. _____

11. When a country can produce a particular good or service at a lower cost than other countries, a(n) (?) exists.   11. _____

12. The (?) is the value of currency in one country compared with the value of currency in another.   12. _____

13. Trade barriers can include (?), tariffs, and embargoes.   13. _____

14. An agreement between two or more companies to work together on a business project is called a(n) (?).   14. _____

15. A(n) (?) is also known as an economic community.   15. _____

Part 3   Matching

Directions   In the Answers column indicate which international trade organization or agreement is best described by each statement.

A.	World Trade Organization (WTO)	C.	North American Free Trade Agreement (NAFTA)
B.	World Bank	D.	International Monetary Fund (IMF)

Answers

16. Maintains a system of world trade and exchange rates   16. _____

17. Created after World War II to provide loans for rebuilding   17. _____

18. Settles trade disputes and enforces free-trade agreements between member countries   18. _____

19. Key function is to provide economic aid to less-developed countries   19. _____

20. Does away with tariffs on goods traded among the member countries   20. _____

Part 4   Activities

21. The currency exchange rate changes constantly based on factors such as a country's balance of payments, economic conditions, and political stability. Figure 3-4 shows the values of currencies in several countries in relation to the U.S. dollar (USD). Visit the website for the Universal Currency Converter at http://www.xe.com/currencyconverter/ and check the value of those currencies today. Fill in the blanks to indicate each currency's units per USD and value in USD. Compare your findings with the values provided in Figure 3-4, and place a check mark in the appropriate blank to indicate whether the value of the USD has increased or decreased in relation to each of the other currencies.

Country	Currency	Units per USD	Value in USD	Increase	Decrease
Britain	pound	_____	_____	_____	_____
Brazil	real	_____	_____	_____	_____
Canada	dollar	_____	_____	_____	_____
European Union	euro	_____	_____	_____	_____
Japan	yen	_____	_____	_____	_____
Saudi Arabia	riyal	_____	_____	_____	_____
South Africa	rand	_____	_____	_____	_____
South Korea	won	_____	_____	_____	_____
Venezuela	bolívar	_____	_____	_____	_____

Activities and Study Guide – Student Edition

22. Numerous items that you buy and use every day are produced in other countries, primarily due to lower production and labor costs. Many American companies maintain manufacturing facilities outside of the United States in order to remain competitive in the marketplace by reducing their costs of production. As more companies move all or part of their business operations outside of the United States, it can have both positive and negative effects on the economies in the United States. as well as in the host country. In the space below, list some of the positive and negative effects on both economies.

Positive Effects on the United States	Negative Effects on the United States
_____	_____
_____	_____
_____	_____
_____	_____

Positive Effects on the Host Country	Negative Effects on the Host Country
_____	_____
_____	_____
_____	_____
_____	_____

23. When it comes to world trade, most people have a strong opinion. Some people believe that too many American jobs are being lost to overseas labor markets. Others believe that international trade actually creates new jobs in the United States. Now that you have completed this chapter, you should better understand the value of international trade, but how do others feel about it? Talk to at least five (5) people you know and ask their opinions. Do not record their names, but bring the results of your survey to class to share. Here are some questions that you might ask.

1. Do you believe there are advantages for the United States in trading with other nations? Why or why not?
2. Do you think international trading increases an understanding of other cultures? If so, how?
3. Do you believe that American jobs are lost because of importing? Why or why not?
4. Do you believe that the North American Free Trade Agreement (NAFTA) and other free trade agreements are good for the U.S. economy? Why or why not?
5. Do you think the United States should place an embargo on certain goods or on goods from certain countries? If so, what goods, what countries, and for what reasons?
6. Do you buy goods made in other countries? If so, what do you buy and why?
7. Do you think it is possible in today's marketplace to only "Buy American"? Why or why not?
8. If you are employed, is your employer involved in international trade? If so, in what way?

[This page left intentionally blank]

Activities and Study Guide – Student Edition

Chapter  4 Study Guide Social Responsibility of Business and Government

Part 1   True or False

Directions   Place a *T* for True or an *F* for False in the Answers column to show whether each of the following statements is true or false.

Answers

1. To be valid and enforceable, contracts must be in writing and signed by both parties.   1._____

2. A logo is a trademark linked with a specific company or product.   2._____

3. The Age Discrimination in Employment Act protects people once they reach age 65.   3._____

4. Intrastate commerce involves companies doing business in only one state.   4._____

5. When a business controls the market for a product or service, it has a monopoly.   5._____

6. Wal-Mart is the single largest employer in the United States.   6._____

7. The government's sole source of income is taxes, such as income, property, and sales taxes.   7._____

8. A business's duty to contribute to the well-being of the community is its social responsibility.   8._____

Part 2   Matching

Directions   In the Answers column, write the letter that represents the word, or group of words, that correctly completes the statement.

Answers

9. Results in an unfair benefit	A. antitrust laws	9._____
10. Cannot be replaced once it has been used up	B. code of ethics	10._____
11. Protects the work of authors, composers, and artists	C. nonrenewable resource	11._____
12. Saves scarce natural resources	D. public utility	12._____
13. Guides the actions of employees	E. copyright	13._____
14. Prevent unfair business practices	F. conservation	14._____
15. Supplies a product or service vital to all people	G. conflict of interest	15._____

Part 3   Multiple Choice

Directions   In the Answers column indicate which government agency is best described by each statement.

A. Environmental Protection Agency (EPA)   C. Small Business Administration (SBA)

B. Department of Commerce   D. Occupational Safety and Health Administration (OSHA)

Answers

16. Regulates safety standards   16._____

17. Monitors and enforces standards for water and air quality   17._____

18. Provides information to help companies make good business decisions   18._____

19. Helps new businesses get started by offering business loans   19._____

20. Works closely with businesses to reduce pollution   20._____

Part 4 Activities

21. Government plays an important role in many areas of society. In Column 1 below are five roles in which government is involved. Column 2 lists several government activities for each role the government plays in the economy. The first item is provided as an example. See if you can add to the list.

COLUMN 1	COLUMN 2
Providing services for members of society	*Example: highways*
	_____
	_____
	_____
Protecting citizens, consumers, businesses, and workers	_____
	_____
	_____
	_____
Regulating utilities and promoting competition	_____
	_____
	_____
	_____
Providing information and support	_____
	_____
	_____
	_____
Buying goods and services	_____
	_____
	_____
	_____

22. Ian Broderick is the president and chief executive officer of a small printing company of about 400 employees. Although the business is small, it has grown steadily over the past few years, and Mr. Broderick and other company executives think it is time to formalize the company's commitment to ethical business practices. You have been asked to write a code of ethics for Broderick Printing Company that will address topics such as honesty, courtesy, and confidentiality as well as rules of conduct for dealing with customers and co-workers. You may want to review the American Express Blue Box Values in Figure 4-1 as a guide. Be sure to give your code of ethics an appropriate title.

_____

_____

_____

_____

_____

_____

_____

_____

_____

_____

_____

23. Employee wellness programs benefit both employers and employees. Healthier workers are more productive and miss fewer days from work due to illness. Conduct a brief survey among people you know who work in various businesses and compile a list of the programs provided by their employers. You may also want to ask them what programs they would like to see offered in the future that currently are not available at their place of employment.

_____

_____

_____

_____

_____

_____

_____

_____

_____

_____

_____

Activities and Study Guide – Student Edition

[This page left intentionally blank]

Activities and Study Guide – Student Edition

Name _____ Class _____ Date _____

Chapter  5 Study Guide Business Organization

Part 1 Agree or Disagree

Directions Indicate whether you agree or disagree with each of the following statements by placing a check mark in the column at the right.

		Agree	Disagree
1.	The most important role of business is to provide employment for people.	_____	_____
2.	Producers use resources to make things that are needed by others.	_____	_____
3.	Service businesses represent the fastest-growing segment of the economy.	_____	_____
4.	Nonprofit corporations do not pay corporate income taxes.	_____	_____
5.	An S corporation is a corporation involved in the service industry.	_____	_____
6.	A mission statement defines what the business wants to achieve.	_____	_____
7.	In a matrix organization structure, work is arranged around business functions.	_____	_____
8.	An organizational chart is a detailed list of job duties and responsibilities.	_____	_____

Part 2 Short Answer

Directions In the Answers column, write the word or words that best describes each statement below.

Answers

9. The large number of people born between 1946 and 1964

9. _____

10. A statement of results a businesses plans to achieve

10. _____

11. Businesses involved in selling goods produced by others

11. _____

12. The number of people assigned to a specific work task and manager

12. _____

13. A business organized by two or more other businesses for a limited time

13. _____

14. Someone who has no contract for long-term employment

14. _____

15. A business owned by members and managed in their interest

15. _____

Part 3 Organizational Structures

Directions In the Answers column, place an F for Functional and an M for Matrix to indicate which organizational structure is best described by each statement.

Answers

16. All people with jobs related to a specific function work together.

16. _____

17. People work with others who have the same skills.

17. _____

18. Assignments may be temporary or long-term.

18. _____

19. People often have little interaction with people in other parts of the business.

19. _____

20. Work is structured around specific projects, products, or customer groups.

20. _____

21. People with varied backgrounds work together to serve the customer.

21. _____

22. Work is arranged within main business functions such as production and marketing.

22. _____

Part 4 Activities

23. Listed below are some statements about the three major forms of business ownership. Place a check mark in the column that identifies the form of business ownership described by each statement. Some statements may apply to more than one type of business ownership.

Characteristics	Sole Proprietorship	Partnership	Corporation
1. Owned and controlled by two or more people	_____	_____	_____
2. A written agreement defines ownership	_____	_____	_____
3. Owned and run by one person	_____	_____	_____
4. Shareholders have a voice in business decisions	_____	_____	_____
5. No protection for personal assets	_____	_____	_____
6. Managed by a board of directors	_____	_____	_____
7. Usually must be dissolved if an owner leaves	_____	_____	_____
8. The easiest form of business to start and run	_____	_____	_____
9. Protects the liability of owners	_____	_____	_____
10. Business income is taxed as personal income	_____	_____	_____
11. Two or more people can invest in the business	_____	_____	_____
12. Must create bylaws or operating procedures	_____	_____	_____
13. Does not require a business name	_____	_____	_____
14. The majority of U.S. businesses	_____	_____	_____
15. Must register the business name and the names of all owners	_____	_____	_____

24. A franchise is a written contract that gives a business the right to sell products and services in a specific way within a given area. A wide variety of familiar businesses within your community operate as franchises, including fast-food restaurants, pizza shops, motels, commercial cleaning companies, and weight loss centers. Select a franchise business and conduct research to learn more about the franchise opportunities.

What start-up costs and franchise fees (percentage of profits) are franchisees required to pay?

_____

What type of operating assistance does the franchiser provide?

_____

What would be the benefits of investing in the franchise instead of starting a similar business on your own?

_____

_____

_____

_____

Activities and Study Guide – Student Edition

25. Each day you deal with many different types of businesses, including producers that create the products and services used by others, intermediaries that sell those goods and services to consumers and businesses, and service businesses that offer intangible activities that are consumed by others. In each of the following scenarios, identify the types of businesses involved.

1. Rob Lopez wants to have three rooms in his home painted. He visits the local Home Depot store, selects the paint colors from samples available in the paint department, and purchases six gallons of Glidden brand paint, which he estimates is sufficient to paint the rooms. After paying for the paint, Rob stops by the service counter and looks at a list of independent painting contractors. He decides to contact several of the contractors to request estimates on painting the rooms.

   _____

   _____

   _____

   _____

   _____

2. Molly Russell loves to cook and has finally turned her hobby into a business by opening Molly's Gourmet Meals, producing complete gourmet meals that are fully cooked and ready to heat and eat. Because she believes in using the finest and freshest ingredients, Molly purchases all of her produce from a small farm close to her home. Molly sells her gourmet meals through various outlets, including the deli departments at several local supermarkets. Because she needs to remain in the kitchen overseeing production, Molly has contracted with another small businessperson, Stephen Daily of Daily Deliveries, to deliver the meals to the supermarkets.

   _____

   _____

   _____

   _____

   _____

3. Jeff Martin owns a mobile dog grooming business, On the Go Grooming, which allows customers the convenience of having their pets groomed at home. Jeff purchased three vans from a local dealership and took them to Custom Car Creations to have sinks, drying stations, and grooming stations added to allow him and his staff to shampoo, dry, and clip dogs right in the customer's driveway. Each van also contains built-in cabinets, which are stocked with an assortment of animal care products that Jeff orders in bulk from the manufacturer. Because many of his customers have begun asking if they can purchase some of the pet care products for use at home, Jeff recently began ordering some of the products in smaller packages to sell to customers.

   _____

   _____

   _____

   _____

   _____

[This page left intentionally blank]

Name _____ Class _____ Date _____

Chapter 6 Study Guide — Entrepreneurship and Small Business Management

Part 1 True or False

Directions Place a *T* for True or an *F* for False in the Answers column to show whether each of the following statements is true or false.

Answers

1. An independent business with 200 employees is considered a small business. 1._____
2. Most new business owners obtain start-up money to finance their business from banks. 2._____
3. Small businesses employ only 10 percent of U.S. workers. 3._____
4. Successful entrepreneurs have many personal characteristics in common. 4._____
5. An entrepreneur is someone who takes a risk by starting his or her own business. 5._____
6. Start-up financing is money needed to pay current operating costs of the business. 6._____
7. One of the main reasons that businesses started by entrepreneurs fail is inadequate capital. 7._____
8. A business plan includes a description of the strengths and weakness of competitors. 8._____

Part 2 Matching

Directions In the Answers column, write the letter that represents the word, or group of words, that correctly matches the statement.

Answers

9. The process of starting, organizing, and managing a business   A. improvement   9._____
10. A brand new invention   B. venture capital   10._____
11. A written description of the business idea   C. mission statement   11._____
12. Money provided by large investors to finance new businesses   D. entrepreneurship   12._____
13. A change that increases the usefulness of a product   E. innovation   13._____

F. business plan

Part 3 Multiple Choice

Directions Identify the type of financing being described by each of the statements by placing a check mark in the correct column.

	Start-up	Short-term	Long-Term
14. Money to pay for current operating costs of the business	_____	_____	_____
15. Purchase of the equipment to open a business	_____	_____	_____
16. Money used to open the business	_____	_____	_____
17. Financing that is obtained for less than a year	_____	_____	_____
18. The license to operate a business	_____	_____	_____
19. Large amounts of money paid over many years	_____	_____	_____
20. The land that the business is built on	_____	_____	_____

Part 4 Activities

21. Many people dream of owning their own business, but only a small percentage of people ever take the risk to become entrepreneurs. As you learned in this chapter, successful entrepreneurs have many personal characteristics in common. Answer each question below by placing a check mark in the *Yes* or *No* column to determine if you have what it takes to become a successful entrepreneur.

	Yes	No
1. I am willing to spend long hours on business ideas that excite me.		
2. I am self-motivated and do not need other people to direct my work.		
3. I am willing to take reasonable risks to achieve my goals.		
4. I am not easily discouraged by failures and learn from my mistakes.		
5. I am well organized and manage my time wisely.		
6. I try to think outside of the box when seeking solutions to problems.		
7. The quality of my work is important to me.		
8. I am willing to seek advice from others who can help and guide me.		
9. I manage money carefully so that I can invest in business ideas.		
10. I have a strong desire to be the best in everything I undertake.		

22. Arrange to interview several small business owners in your community. Prepare your list of questions prior to conducting the interviews. You may want to ask how they decided on the product or service they offer. What background or experience did they have prior to starting the business? How did they initially finance the business? What kind of research did they conduct? Compare their responses. What similarities and differences do you notice among the people that you interviewed?

_____

_____

_____

_____

_____

_____

23. Many small businesses fail because the owners have a good idea for a business, but they fail to establish a written plan to cover all of the major business activities. Investigate a business that you might like to start. By referring to the Elements of a Business Plan in Chapter 6, begin drafting a written plan for your new business. You will need to include a complete description of the business as well as a description of any competitors you might have. Your business plan also should analyze your customers and describe the operations and marketing plans for the business. Finally, your business plan should analyze your financial needs, both for starting and for growing the business.

_____

_____

_____

_____

_____

_____

Activities and Study Guide – Student Edition

Name _____ Class _____ Date _____

Chapter  7 Study Guide   Management and Leadership

Part 1 Yes or No

Directions   Indicate your answer to each of the following questions by placing a
check mark on the line under *yes* or *no* at the right.   **Yes**   **No**

1. Are planning, staffing, and controlling all functions of management?   _____ _____
2. Is communication with suppliers an example of internal communication?   _____ _____
3. Are core values guiding principles of the company?   _____ _____
4. Is it true that "Leaders are born and not made"?   _____ _____
5. Is strategic management a style in which the manager is more controlling?   _____ _____
6. Are middle managers responsible for specific areas of operation in a business?   _____ _____
7. Do ethical business practices involve only the company's executives?   _____ _____
8. Is communication from one manager to another horizontal communication?   _____ _____

Part 2 Unscramble

Directions   Unscramble the following vocabulary words that were discussed in
Chapter 7.   **Answers**

9. louvcarese (2 words)   9. _____

10. funceelni   10. _____

11. dearpilshe   11. _____

12. stiche   12. _____

13. gametannem   13. _____

14. thanimureolans (2 words)   14. _____

15. ginlapnn   15. _____

Part 3 Matching

Directions   In the Answers column indicate which kind of influence is best
described by each statement.

A. position influence   C. expert influence

B. reward influence   D. identity influence   **Answers**

16. Other employees acknowledge that the person has specialized knowledge.   16. _____

17. Examples include money, job benefits, or recognition.   17. _____

18. Having authority over others results in positive responses to requests.   18. _____

19. Criticizing rather than praising employees is another way to exercise influence.   19. _____

20. Employees are more willing to support someone whom they trust and respect.   20. _____

Part 4 Activities

21. Most leaders possess characteristics that make them effective managers. Each of those leadership characteristics offers a benefit to employees. Below is a list of the characteristics of effective leaders that were discussed in this chapter. For each characteristic, write a statement describing how employees will benefit from their manager having that specific characteristic.

Understanding _____

Initiative _____

Dependability _____

Judgment _____

Objectivity _____

Confidence _____

Stability _____

Cooperation _____

Honesty _____

Courage _____

Communication _____

Intelligence _____

22. Visit the website for any large company and review its section on corporate ethics. Make a list of the ethical concerns and situations that are specifically addressed in the document. How could the document be improved, in your opinion?

_____

_____

_____

_____

_____

_____

_____

23. Arrange to "shadow" a manager at a local company and observe the various tasks that the manager performs during the workday. Take notes during your visit and compile a list of each activity in which the manager is involved. From your notes, prepare a report linking each observed activity with one of the five functions of management—planning, organizing, staffing, implementing, or controlling. Also, identify the management style(s) you observed the manager using throughout the day. If you observed more than one style, describe the circumstances in which each style was used.

Name _____ Class _____ Date _____

Chapter  8 Study Guide Human Resources, Culture, and Diversity

Part 1 Agree or Disagree

Directions Indicate whether you agree or disagree with each of the following statements by placing a check mark in the column at the right.

	Agree	Disagree
1. A blue-collar worker is employed in an office with a casual dress code.		F
2. A layoff is a type of termination due to a change in business conditions.	T	
3. A cafeteria plan is an employee benefit involving company-paid meals.	T	
4. A glass ceiling is an architectural style that provides an open look for offices.		F
5. Downsizing is designed to decrease costs and increase efficiency.	T	
6. Family leave policies permit employees to take off for a birth or adoption.	T	
7. Flextime allows employees flexibility in the time they begin and end work.	T	
8. A permanent employee works in the same position for his or her entire career.		F

Part 2 Completion

Directions In the Answers column, write the word or words needed to complete each sentence.

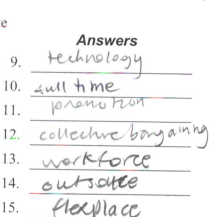

Answers

9. (?) involves the use of automation to increase productivity. 9. technology

10. A work schedule of 30 or more hours describes a (?) employee. 10. full time

11. When an employee receives a (?), she assumes more responsibility. 11. promotion

12. Formal negotiation between management and unions is known as (?). 12. collective bargaining

13. People 16 and older who are employed or seeking work make up the (?). 13. workforce

14. Many jobs in the United States are (?) to other countries to save money. 14. outsource

15. Telecommuting is a popular form of (?). 15. flexplace

Part 3 Forms of Compensation

Directions Indicate the type of compensation described by each statement by placing a check mark in the appropriate column at the right. (There may be more than one correct answer for each statement.)

	Time Wage	Straight Salary	Incentive Pay	Benefits
16. Employees receive a share of company profits.				✓
17. An employee is paid $7.50 per hour worked.	✓			
18. A salesperson earns 10% of his or her total sales.			✓	
19. A clerk receives $500 per week plus paid vacation.		✓		✓
20. Employees earn $0.30 for each widget produced.			✓	

Part 4 Activities

21. Companies today offer a variety of fringe benefits to employees. Each benefit offers value to employees. Some businesses allow employees to select benefits that meet their specific needs by using a cafeteria plan. Below is a list of common fringe benefits. For each benefit, write a statement that describes the value of the benefit to employees.

Fringe Benefit	Value to Employees
Vacation time	mental health, freed schedule
Health insurance	security, free insurance, health
Life insurance	Security, no need to pay for insurance
Employee savings plan	Security, financially helps
Paid sick days	Saves money, security
Flextime	Gives freedom of schedule
Retirement program	Gives them security
Recreational facility	Helps stay fit + mental health
Day care for employees' children	Helps them spend more time at work, less cost for day care/childcare
Employee discount for store purchases	Helps them purchase more/higher quality

Which of the fringe benefits listed above would be most important to you? Why?

I would want health + life insurance, as well as paid sick days because those would minimize expenses in a very expensive field.

22. Conduct research on one of the following federal laws that relate to human resources: Family and Medical Leave Act, Civil Rights Act of 1964, Age Discrimination and Employment Act of 1967, or Americans with Disabilities Act. Organize and present information on the law you have selected by preparing a PowerPoint presentation, poster, or other creative representation of the material.

23. Select a job in which you may be interested. Determine the requirements for obtaining employment in that position by reviewing the classified advertisements in one or more newspapers for a period of at least one week. How many jobs in your chosen field are advertised? What are the listed requirements for each position? Do most of the ads list the same or similar job requirements (such as education or prior work experience)? Visit the U.S. Bureau of Labor Statistics website to locate employment projections for the position. If possible, also visit a job or career fair to learn more about job opportunities in your chosen position. Compile your research in a report that provides a detailed overview of the job opportunities in the position you have selected.

Activities and Study Guide – Student Edition

Name _____ Class _____ Date _____

Chapter  9 Study Guide   Career Planning and Development

Part 1   True or False

Directions   Place a *T* for True or an *F* for False in the Answers column to show whether each of the following statements is true or false.

Answers

1. Scholarships, student loans, and work-study options are all types of financial aid programs.
2. Abilities are natural, inborn aptitudes to do specific things.
3. Work-related experience can be gained through volunteer and school activities.
4. Informational interviews help you learn about specific careers by talking to workers.
5. An experience-based resume highlights your abilities related to the job you are pursuing.
6. If you expressed your appreciation during the interview, a follow-up letter is not necessary.
7. Mobility is often necessary to pursue your chosen career.
8. Your résumé should always include a list of references.

1._____
2._____
3._____
4._____
5._____
6._____
7._____
8._____

Part 2   Matching

Directions   In the Answers column, write the letter that represents the word, or group of words, that correctly completes the statement.

Answers

9. Spending a day or week with a worker to learn about a job
10. Asks for employment-related information
11. An experienced employee who acts as a counselor
12. Things that are important to you
13. Provides evidence of your ability and skills
14. Talking to other people about their jobs
15. Being able to perform a mental or physical task

A. values
B. networking
C. ability
D. career portfolio
E. job shadow
F. mentor
G. application form
H. résumé

9._____
10._____
11._____
12._____
13._____
14._____
15._____

Part 3   Types of Interviews

Directions   Indicate the type of interview described by each statement by placing a check mark in the appropriate column at the right. (There may be more than one correct answer for each statement.)

	Informational Interview	Employment Interview	Exit Interview
16. Prepare in advance for questions you might be asked.	_____	_____	_____
17. Learn more about the preparation needed for a career.	_____	_____	_____
18. Answer questions honestly and completely.	_____	_____	_____
19. Offer constructive feedback.	_____	_____	_____
20. Thank the interviewer for his or her time and for the opportunity to discuss the job.	_____	_____	_____

Part 4   Activities

21. Because your values affect your career plans directly or indirectly, it is a good idea to examine the personal values you hold. Read each value described in the list below. Then place a check mark in the column at the right that indicates the importance of that value to you.

IMPORTANCE TO ME

VALUE	Very Important	Important	Not Important
Prestige—gaining recognition and status	_____	_____	_____
Money—getting financial reward	_____	_____	_____
Power—having control over people, money, or things	_____	_____	_____
Achievement—accomplishing goals	_____	_____	_____
Independence—controlling your time and actions	_____	_____	_____
Security—having a stable work condition	_____	_____	_____
Belonging—feeling you are part of a group	_____	_____	_____
Serving others—doing things for others	_____	_____	_____

List the three values you consider to be most important to you. State how each of these values might affect your career choice.

_____

_____

_____

22. When applying for certain jobs, you may be required to complete the company's standard application form. For other jobs, however, you may need to provide the potential employer with a résumé. Begin compiling relevant information that could be used to construct your résumé, such as a statement of your career objective, education, work or volunteer experience, and any honors you have earned or activities in which you are involved. Once you have assembled all of the necessary information, prepare your résumé using the sample résumé in this chapter as a guide.

_____

_____

_____

23. Review the list of common interview questions in this chapter, and write answers for each of the questions. Make an audio recording of your answers. Play the recording and listen for answers that are not delivered in a clear, positive tone. Record those answers again and continue working to improve your delivery until you feel that you could answer each question confidently in an actual interview.

_____

_____

_____

Activities and Study Guide – Student Edition

DECISIONS, DECISIONS, DECISIONS—PART 1

A Decision-Making Project

As a consumer, worker, and citizen, you constantly make decisions that affect your future—both personally and financially. Some of these decisions are made quickly; others require time, research, and careful deliberation.

In this project, you will make various personal and business decisions, based on your personal goals, values, and business knowledge. Each situation you will consider presents several choices you can make, but each choice will have financial consequences. Therefore, you should choose carefully. Random events that are based on chance also will affect you financially. The components of this project are:

DECISIONS: For each decision, you will have three alternatives from which to choose. You should consider not only the immediate effects of your decision but also how it will affect your future.

CONSEQUENCES: These are direct results of the decisions you will be making. Your teacher will provide you with the consequences as they are needed.

RANDOM EVENTS: Random events are beyond your control. However, they still can affect your financial situation. Cut out the numbered slips of paper below and place them in a bag or box. When instructed to do so, you will draw a number that will indicate how you will be affected by the random event.

After you have made your decision for each situation, you will record the financial result on the summary sheet at the end of the project. Each decision, consequence, or random event will either increase or decrease your balance. At the end of the project, calculate your final balance.

Your teacher will assign you to work individually or in a group. If you are assigned to work in a group, you should discuss your decisions with other group members and arrive at a shared decision.

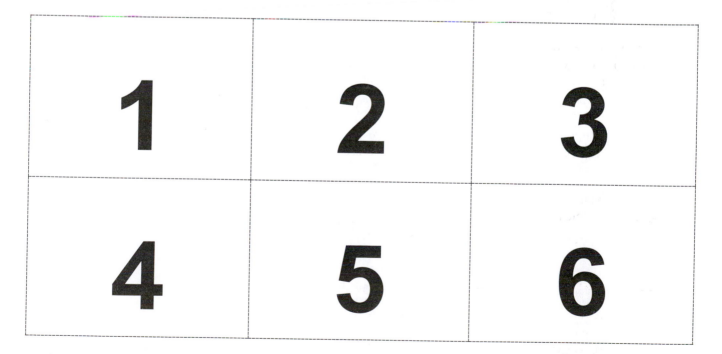

Procedures

1. Review the decision-making steps in Chapter 1 of the textbook.
2. Encourage students to consider all factors affecting their decisions rather than making selections based on the immediate payoff.
3. Assign students to work individually or in teams.
4. Remind students that after each situation they must record an increase or decrease on the summary sheet.

Instructional Approach

Students can be assigned to work individually or as part of a team. Each team may consist of two to four members. If students are assigned to work in teams, they must discuss each decision and form a team decision. If a team approach is used, each team should use only one summary sheet.

Additional Suggestions

- Require students to conduct outside research before making some of the decisions.
- Ask students to discuss their decisions with parents or others before they make them.
- Review business terms and concepts to make sure students have a clear understanding.
- Discuss career opportunities related to some of the situations in the project.
- Use student helpers to provide results of consequences to individuals or groups.
- If available, dice present a more streamlined method of generating random numbers one through six than do slips of papers.

Required Time

The time needed for this project can vary from one to four class sessions depending on the length of the class period and the time used for discussion. Time will be needed to introduce students to the format and procedures of the project. In addition, follow-up questions are provided for post-simulation discussion.

Evaluation Techniques

Because correct answers vary, a grade of "complete" or "incomplete" is probably most appropriate. In addition, students can be evaluated based on math accuracy, class discussion of situations, and interpersonal relations when working with other students.

To help students evaluate their own performance, pose some of the follow-up questions. You may also wish to ask students if they were able to follow the decision-making process outlined in Chapter 1. Were their decisions overly influenced by the monetary payoff? If they worked in groups, did all group members participate in the decisions? Through such questioning, you will enable students to see that there is a methodical way of approaching decision making, despite the many, sometimes unknown, factors affecting their decisions.

Activities and Study Guide – Student Edition

Name _____ Class _____ Date _____

Situation 1—Decision—After High School

You have graduated from high school and must decide what you will do next. Keep in mind that your decision will affect future opportunities. Record the amount for your decision on your summary sheet.

Choice A	Choice B	Choice C
continue your education and work part-time	work full time at a local business	start your own business

Situation 2—Decision—Rent or Buy

You need to choose a place to live. You have a choice of renting or buying. Before you make your decision, you should investigate the advantages and disadvantages of each choice.

Choice A	Choice B	Choice C
rent an apartment, which requires a security deposit and first month's rent	buy a previously owned house, which requires a down payment	buy a new condominium, which requires a down payment

Situation 3—Random Event—Supply and Demand in Action

Due to recent economic conditions, the supply and/or demand of various products has changed. Select a number to determine which result affects you and record the amount on your summary sheet.

Result 1	Result 2	Result 3	Result 4	Result 5	Result 6
lower taxes, higher demand (prices up)	higher taxes, lower demand (prices down)	bad weather, reduced supply	new technology, increased supply	high government spending, increased demand	higher wages, higher demand

Activities and Study Guide – Student Edition

Situation 4—Decision—Selecting a Computer

Your business and personal needs require the use of a computer. Select a method for obtaining the use of a computer.

Choice A	Choice B	Choice C
purchase computer with monthly payment of	rent computer with monthly charge of	buy computer time from information processing service bureau for a monthly charge of

Situation 5—Consequence—A Previous Decision

As a result of your decision in Situation 1, you will receive a salary increase. The amount of this increase must be obtained from your teacher. Be sure to record the amount of the increase on your summary sheet.

Situation 6—Random Event—Moving Expenses

Your recent move into a new home has resulted in various expenses—utility deposits, kitchen supplies, and linens. Select a number to determine which result will affect you and record the amount on your summary sheet.

Result 1	Result 2	Result 3	Result 4	Result 5	Result 6

Situation 7—Decision—A Vote on Taxes

Your local government needs additional revenue for various community services. Carefully consider your options, and select one of the choices below.

Choice A	Choice B	Choice C
vote for a tax increase, which would maintain all current public services	vote for a tax increase, which would maintain roads and schools at current levels but could result in a decrease in other public services	vote against a tax increase, which could result in a decrease in numerous public services

Situation 8—Random Event—Interest Rates

Interest rates are always changing. Select a number to determine how the change in interest rates will affect you. Record the results on your summary sheet.

Result 1	Result 2	Result 3	Result 4	Result 5	Result 6
increased money supply, rates fall	lower money supply, rates rise	increased demand for loans, rates rise	lower demand for loans, rates fall	higher wages and spending, rates rise	decreased government borrowing, rates fall

Situation 9—Decision—Additional Career Training

You must decide whether you will pursue additional education. Record your choice on your summary sheet.

Choice A	Choice B	Choice C
obtain advanced training in your chosen career	obtain training in another career area with a good occupational outlook for the future	obtain no additional training at this time

Situation 10—Consequence—Computer Costs

As a result of your decision in Situation 4, your computer costs have been influenced by various factors. See your teacher for the results of this situation. Be sure to record the amount on your summary sheet.

Situation 11—Random Event—Salary Increase

As a result of your time and effort on the job, you qualify for a pay increase. Select a number to determine the amount. Record the results on your summary sheet.

Result 1	Result 2	Result 3	Result 4	Result 5	Result 6

Situation 12—Decision—Product Purchase

You have decided to buy a television for your new home. Choose one of the following and record its cost on your summary sheet. You may want to investigate each option carefully before making your decision.

Choice A	Choice B	Choice C
a well-known national brand	a store brand	an unknown brand

Situation 13—Random Event—Computer Time Savings

As a result of recent developments, a cost savings has been created related to your computer. Select a number to determine the amount of the savings. Record the results on your summary sheet.

Result 1	Result 2	Result 3	Result 4	Result 5	Result 6

Situation 14—Consequence—Home Repair

The driveway of your home is in need of repair. Based on the decision you made in Situation 2, obtain the amount of this repair from your teacher. Be sure to record the amount of the increase on your summary sheet.

Activities and Study Guide – Student Edition

Situation 15—Decision—Foreign Trade

The company for which you work must decide where it wants to expand sales. You must make the decision.

Choice A	Choice B	Choice C
expand foreign business, maintain current level of domestic business	expand level of domestic operations; no foreign business	expand both foreign and domestic business operations

Situation 16—Consequence—Training Results

As a result of your decision in Situation 9, your salary level has been affected. See your teacher for the results of this situation. Be sure to record the amount on your summary sheet.

Situation 17—Decision—New Career Choice

You are considering a career change. There are costs associated with moving and training expenses. Record your choice on the summary sheet.

Choice A	Choice B	Choice C
select a new career in a field related to your present job	select a new career in a different field of work	maintain the same career as presently held

Situation 18—Random Event—Changing Government Services

Because of economic conditions, government tax revenues have decreased and some government services have been reduced. Consumers must now pay for some services that were previously provided. Select a number to determine how you will be affected.

Result 1	Result 2	Result 3	Result 4	Result 5	Result 6

Situation 19—Consequence—Television Repair

The television you purchased in Situation 12 is in need of repair. See your teacher for the costs involved. Be sure to record the amount on your summary sheet.

Situation 20—Decision—Store Choice

You have decided to purchase your clothing on a regular basis at one of the types of stores listed. Record your choice on your summary sheet.

Choice A	Choice B	Choice C
full-service department store located 8 miles away	full-service local specialty store located 3 miles away	factory outlet located 13 miles away

Situation 21—Consequence—Computer Repair

Due to heavy usage, the computer you selected in Situation 4 needs to be repaired. See your teacher for the results of this situation. Record the amount on your summary sheet.

Situation 22—Decision—Type of Business Organization

You have decided to start your own business. Now you must decide which of the three basic business structures you will use. Record your choice on your summary sheet.

Choice A	Choice B	Choice C
sole proprietorship with organizational costs of	partnership with organizational costs of	corporation with organizational costs of

Activities and Study Guide – Student Edition

Situation 23—Consequence—Clothing Costs

As a result of your decision in Situation 20, obtain the amount of your clothing costs from your teacher. Be sure to record the amount on your summary sheet.

Situation 24—Random Event—Economic Conditions

As a result of a depressed economy, you are unemployed for a length of time. Select a number to determine the amount of salary you have lost. Record the results on your summary sheet.

Result 1	Result 2	Result 3	Result 4	Result 5	Result 6

Situation 25—Consequence—Government Costs

Certain government services have been affected by the recent tax vote in Situation 7. See your teacher for the results. Be sure to record the amount on your summary sheet.

Situation 26—Random Event—Profit or Loss

Your involvement with a business in Situation 22 has resulted in a profit or loss. To determine which you will receive, select a number. Record the results on your summary sheet.

Result 1	Result 2	Result 3	Result 4	Result 5	Result 6

Activities and Study Guide – Student Edition

Situation 27—Consequence—Housing Equity

See your teacher regarding increased value of your property resulting from your decision in Situation 2. Record the amount on your summary sheet.

Situation 28—Consequence—New Career Success

See your teacher regarding a possible salary increase resulting from your career decision in Situation 17. Record the amount on your summary sheet.

Situation 29—Consequence—Business Ownership and Expansion

See your teacher regarding the results of your choices made in Situations 15 and 22.

Activities and Study Guide – Student Edition

DECISIONS, DECISIONS, DECISIONS—PART 1—SUMMARY SHEET

	SITUATION	TOPIC	CHOICE	AMOUNT	BALANCE
1.	Decision	After High School	A	+ 7,000	7,000
2.	Decision	Rent or Buy	C	− 2600	4,400
3.	Random Event	Supply and Demand in Action	3	− 120	4280
4.	Decision	Selecting a Computer	A	− 150	4130
5.	Consequence	A Previous Decision		+ 2000	6130
6.	Random Event	Moving Expenses	3	− 120	6010
7.	Decision	A Vote on Taxes	A	− 200	5,810
8.	Random Event	Interest Rates	4	+/− +80	5890
9.	Decision	Additional Career Training	B	− 960	4990
10.	Consequence	Computer Costs		+/− −60	4930
11.	Random Event	Salary Increase	2	+ 50	4980
12.	Decision	Product Purchase	A	− 600	5580
13.	Random Event	Computer Time Savings	3	+ 90	5670
14.	Consequence	Home Repair		− 0	5670
15.	Decision	Foreign Trade	B	− 300	5370
16.	Consequence	Training Results		+ 2100	7470
17.	Decision	New Career Choice	A	− 400	7070
18.	Random Event	Changing Government Services	1	− 20	7050
19.	Consequence	Television Repair		− 20	7030
20.	Decision	Store Choice	A	− 70	6060
21.	Consequence	Computer Repair		− $20	6060 5940
22.	Decision	Type of Business Organization	C	− 500	5440
23.	Consequence	Clothing Costs		− 100	4440
24.	Random Event	Economic Conditions	5	− 440	4000
25.	Consequence	Government Costs		− 0	4000
26.	Random Event	Profit or Loss	3	+/− 550	3450
27.	Consequence	Housing Equity		+ 800	4250
28.	Consequence	New Career Success		+ 1200	5650
29.	Consequence	Business Ownership and Expansion	(a)	+ 650	6300
			(b)	− 950	5350

FINAL BALANCE 5350

Student Comments

1. Which decisions might you have made differently? Why?

2. What factors did you forget to consider when making a decision?

3. What advice would you give to someone about making financial decisions?

Name _____ Class _____ Date _____

Chapter 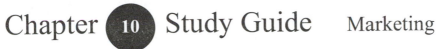 10 Study Guide   Marketing

Part 1 Yes or No

Directions Indicate your answer to each of the following questions by placing a
check mark on the line under *yes* or *no* at the right.

		Yes	**No**
1.	Is marketing non-paid promotional communication presented by the media?	_____	_____
2.	Is a marketing mix the blending of product, distribution, price, and promotion?	_____	_____
3.	Does a focus group involve observing the actions of consumers?	_____	_____
4.	Is it easier to control the quality of a service than the quality of a product?	_____	_____
5.	Does convenience affect the price consumers are willing to pay for a product?	_____	_____
6.	Is a product's route from the producer to the consumer its stream of revenue?	_____	_____
7.	Does personal selling always involve face-to-face contact with the customer?	_____	_____
8.	Is mass promotion less expensive than personalized promotion?	_____	_____

Part 2 Short Answer

Directions In the Answers column, write the word or words that best describes
each statement below.

Answers

9. Setting and communicating the value of products and services   9. _____

10. A unique identification for a company's products   10. _____

11. An activity consumed at the same time it is produced   11. _____

12. A specific group of consumers with similar wants and needs   12. _____

13. An amount added to the cost of a product to establish the selling price   13. _____

14. Communication used to inform, persuade, or remind   14. _____

Part 3 Buying Motives

Directions Place a check mark in the correct column to identify the type of buying motive
being described by each of the purchases listed below.

		Emotional	**Rational**
15.	Engagement ring	_____	_____
16.	Concert tickets	_____	_____
17.	New refrigerator	_____	_____
18.	Birthday cake and party supplies	_____	_____
19.	Hybrid car that gets 65 miles to a gallon of gas	_____	_____
20.	Mortgage lender	_____	_____
21.	Hawaiian vacation	_____	_____

Activities and Study Guide – Student Edition

41

Part 4   Activities

22. Businesses carefully study consumers' wants and needs and their previous experience with products and services to identify the best target market. The first column below lists examples of products that will fit the needs of a specific target market. The second column lists people in a particular target market. In the Answers column, match each product with the most appropriate target market by writing the letter of the target market.

Products	Target Market	Answers
1. Foreign language audio lessons	a. someone expecting a baby	_____
2. Graphing calculator	b. new homeowner	_____
3. Grocery store-brand food items	c. 6-year-old child	_____
4. Car seat	d. business executive traveling abroad	_____
5. Lawnmower	e. culinary school student	_____
6. Minivan	f. couple planning a vacation	_____
7. Action figure lunch box	g. high school advanced math student	_____
8. Set of knives	h. family of 5 with a busy schedule	_____
9. 4-wheel-drive truck	i. person who hauls lumber	_____
10. Set of matching luggage	j. family on a budget	_____

23. One of the seven key functions of marketing is promotion. Study current ads in your local newspaper and clip the ads that offer special promotions. Examples might include offers such as "buy one, get one free" at a grocery store. Create a poster to display the ads you found illustrating the various forms of promotion. Do you think these promotional offers influence customers' buying decisions? Why or why not?

_____

_____

_____

_____

_____

24. Publicity is a different form of promotion from advertising. Companies design their own advertising and pay to present it through various outlets to their target markets. Publicity is promotional communication that is presented by the media. There is no cost to the company. Most publicity, however, must have some type of newsworthy angle. Examples might include a company's participation in an event to raise money for a charity, employees of a company volunteering to clean up a local park, or business news, such as a company creating a new product or expanding into a new market. Search through current newspapers or business magazines and locate an article that provides publicity about an organization. What is the activity described in the article that provides a newsworthy angle to the information?

_____

_____

_____

_____

_____

Activities and Study Guide – Student Edition

Name _____ Class _____ Date _____

Chapter  11 Study Guide   Business and Technology

Part 1   Agree or Disagree

Directions   Indicate whether you agree or disagree with each of the following
statements by placing a check mark in the column at the right.

		Agree	*Disagree*
1.	The physical elements of a computer system are called the hardware.	_____	_____
2.	Computer language uses a system of letters, words, numbers, and symbols.	_____	_____
3.	Displaced workers are those who have been transferred to a new location.	_____	_____
4.	Despite advances in technology, robots exist only in science fiction movies.	_____	_____
5.	A company's private computer network is called an intranet.	_____	_____
6.	Video conferencing allows people in different locations to "meet" by satellite.	_____	_____
7.	The keyboard is the control center of a computer system.	_____	_____
8.	Thieves who get information online about a person commit identify theft.	_____	_____

Part 2   Completion

Directions   In the Answers column, write the word or words needed to complete
each of the following sentences.

Answers

9. The (?) is the largest and best-known computer network in the world.   9. _____

10. Programs that perform specific tasks, such as accounting, are known as (?).   10. _____

11. Conducting business using the Internet or other technology is called (?).   11. _____

12. The use of (?) allows computers to reason, learn, and make decisions.   12. _____

13. Workers who are involved in (?) use a computer at home to do their job.   13. _____

14. A (?) is code hidden in a system that can damage software or stored data.   14. _____

Part 3   Matching

Directions   In the Answers column, write the letter that represents the word, or group of
words, that correctly completes the statement.

Answers

15.	Using technology to create product styles and designs	A. spreadsheet software	15. _____
16.	Programs that help solve technical problems	B. piracy	16. _____
17.	Software that performs calculations	C. operating system software	17. _____
18.	Translates commands and allows application programs to interact with the computer's hardware	D. computer-aided design	18. _____
19.	Stealing or illegally copying software or information	E. expert systems	19. _____
20.	Stores data such as account balance and credit history	F. database software	20. _____
		G. smart card	

Part 4 Activities

21. With more and more personal and confidential information being stored in computer files and databases, the crime of identify theft has become a growing concern. If thieves are able to obtain enough personal information about you, they can apply for credit accounts in your name and even withdraw money from your bank accounts. They can and do ruin the credit ratings of innocent people. The damage sometimes takes years to undo. Conduct research on the topic of identity theft, and locate at least three recent articles. Using word processing software, prepare a brochure that provides up-to-date information about the crime of identity theft and advises consumers on ways to protect themselves from becoming a victim.

_____

_____

_____

_____

_____

_____

22. Numerous health issues and concerns have arisen as a result of the shift to a more technology-oriented workforce. Find several articles that deal with the health-related issues of working on a computer. List the major health concerns and suggest ways that they might be alleviated. For example, poor posture or back pain could be the result of a poorly adjusted chair. The solution could be as simple as adjusting the height of the chair or purchasing a newer, more ergonomically designed chair.

_____

_____

_____

_____

_____

_____

23. Technology is so integral to our everyday lives that often we fail to think about the things it allows us to do more easily and efficiently. With a small group of other students, brainstorm a list of everyday activities made easier by technology.

_____

_____

_____

_____

_____

_____

Activities and Study Guide – Student Edition

Chapter  12 Study Guide   Financial Management

Part 1   True or False

Directions   Place a *T* for True or an *F* for False in the Answers column to show whether each of the following statements is true or false.

Answers

1. Most start-up businesses can be opened with a minimum of expenditures.
2. Financial records provide detailed information about the financial activities of a company.
3. Owners' equity is the value of the business after liabilities are subtracted from assets.
4. An income statement usually covers a five-year period.
5. The income that a business receives over a period of time is called profits.
6. When expenses are greater than income, a net loss occurs.
7. Financial performance ratios compare a company's financial elements to its competitors.
8. With direct deposit, net pay is transferred electronically into the employee's bank account.

1._____
2._____
3._____
4._____
5._____
6._____
7._____
8._____

Part 2   Identifying Financial Records

Directions   In the Answers column, write the letter that represents the word, or group of words, that correctly identifies each type of financial record.

Answers

9. The type and number of products on hand for sale
10. Credit purchases made by customers
11. The amount assets have decreased in value due to age or use
12. Information on employees, their compensation, and benefits
13. The buildings and equipment owned by the business
14. All taxes collected, owed, and paid
15. Companies from which credit purchases were made

A. asset records
B. depreciation records
C. inventory records
D. accounts receivable
E. accounts payable
F. cash records
G. payroll records
H. tax records

9. _____
10. _____
11. _____
12. _____
13. _____
14. _____
15. _____

Part 3   Unscramble

Directions   Unscramble the following vocabulary words that were discussed in Chapter 12.   **Answers**

16. yalplor
17. tasess
18. tubdeg
19. nablacheets (2 words)
20. neverue
21. tilebiliais
22. pexnesse

16. _____
17. _____
18. _____
19. _____
20. _____
21. _____
22. _____

Part 4   Activities

23. Financial statements are reports that summarize the financial performance of a business. The balance sheet lists the assets, liabilities, and owner's equity of the business. In the balance sheet below, some information is missing. Complete the balance sheet by calculating the missing amounts.

Countryside Bicycle Shop

Balance Sheet

December 31, 20xx

Assets:		Liabilities:	
Cash	$38,425	Accounts payable	$30,070
Accounts receivable		Notes payable	$28,695
Supplies	$12,675	Loans payable	
Equipment	$16,300	Total liabilities:	$71,415
		Owner's Equity:	
Total Assets:	$82,200	Total liabilities and owner's equity:	

24. Visit the website of a publicly held company, such as P&G or Hewlett-Packard, and view the most recent annual report. What type of financial information is provided in the company's annual report? What is the value to investors of having this kind of information? Can you tell from the annual report how the company is performing?

25. A company's income statement reports revenues, expenses, and net income or loss from the business operations for a specified period of time, usually six months or one year. Review the income statement for The Unique Boutique women's clothing store and answer the questions below.

The Unique Boutique

Income Statement

For the 6-month Period Ending June 30, 20xx

Operating Revenue		*Operating Expenses*	
Cash sales	$15,825	Salaries and wages	$12,500
Credit/charge sales	$18,940	Advertising	$875
Total operating revenue	$34,765	Rent	$2,000
		Utilities	$750
		Supplies	$695
		Other	$350
		Total operating expenses	$17,170

Did the Unique Boutique earn a profit or a loss during this period? How much?

_____

_____

Name _____ Class _____ Date _____

Chapter  13 Study Guide   Production and Business Operations

Part 1   Completion

Directions   In the Answers column, write the word or words that best completes each statement below.

Answers

1. Building a unique product to meet the needs of one customer   _____

2. Best practices among all competitors   _____

3. Goods arrive when needed for production, use, or sale   _____

4. Products are obtained from nature or grown from natural resources   _____

5. A specific measurement against which an activity or result is judged   _____

6. Using short production runs to produce a precise amount of a product   _____

Part 2   Multiple Choice

Directions   In the Answers column, write the letter that represents the word, or group of words, that correctly matches the statement.

Answers

7. The three categories of products used by businesses and consumers are natural resources, agricultural products, and (a) custom-produced goods (b) processed goods (c) synthetic goods (d) extracted goods.   7._____

8. Continuous process improvement (a) increases the quality of work (b) reduces errors and waste (c) monitors performance continuously (d) all of the above.   8._____

9. Another term for logistics is (a) inventory productions management (b) storage facilities management (c) supply chain management (a) acquisitions management.   9._____

10. Research conducted to discover new solutions to problems without having a specific product in mind is called (a) applied research (b) pure research (c) unstructured research (d) natural research.   10._____

11. An assembly process that makes a large number of identical products using a continuous procedure is (a) mass production (b) custom production (c) continuous processing (d) intermittent processing.   11._____

Part 3   Yes or No

Directions   Indicate your answer to each of the following questions by placing a check mark on the line under *yes* or *no* at the right.

Answers

	Yes	No
12. Does processing involve improving the form of another product?	_____	_____
13. Is training one of the less important human resource activities?	_____	_____
14. Is a schedule a time plan for completing operating activities?	_____	_____
15. Does manufacturing always involve large, complex building plans?	_____	_____

Part 4   Activities

16. Arrange to tour a manufacturing facility in your community so that you can observe the manufacturing process that takes place as raw materials or parts are converted into finished products. Then create a visual representation of the process you observed. Be sure to include each step involved in the manufacturing process.

17. To remain competitive, companies are continuously working to design new products or to improve existing products to meet consumer needs and wants. Some of the products you may regularly use today may not even have been invented until a few short years ago. Select a product and conduct research to learn how it was invented. Then create a timeline illustrating the improvements in the product up to the present time. For example, if you choose to illustrate the improvements in music recordings, you might develop a timeline that goes from the first hand-powered phonograph to today's MP3 players. After you have created your timeline, use your imagination to suggest an improvement that could be made in the product design that could become the "next generation" for that product category.

18. Facilities managers are responsible for maintaining the buildings in which a business is located. They must keep the building in good working order to provide a clean, safe environment for employees as well as visitors. Depending on the size of the company, they also may oversee a variety of other vital functions. Arrange to interview the facilities manager at a business in your community. Prepare a list of questions in advance that you would like to ask. After you have conducted the interview, write a report describing the duties of the facilities manager and how the activities affect the operation of the business.

19. Many businesses, including retail shops, restaurants, and hotels, employ the services of mystery shoppers or secret shoppers to visit their facilities "undercover" and provide reports on how well the business is doing. Select a local retail business and visit that business as if you were a typical customer. Then prepare a report that addresses the following questions. Include suggestions on how the business might improve the facility to attract more customers.

   • Was the parking lot well maintained? Was it free of litter? Were the parking spaces clearly marked?

   • Was the outside of the building clean? Were the outside signs fully lit and in good repair? Were the doors and windows free of dirt and handprints?

   • Was the inside clean and well lit? If the floors were carpeted, was the carpet free of dirt and stains?

   • Were racks and shelves fully stocked with merchandise? Was there room to move freely among the racks of merchandise?

   • Were the fitting rooms clean? Was merchandise regularly returned to the sales floor instead of left in the fitting rooms?

   • Was the store environment appealing—temperature, lighting, air quality, music, and so on?

   • Was there an adequate number of salespeople available to help customers and answer questions?

   • Were cash registers fully staffed so that customers did not have to wait in long lines to check out?

   • Were the restrooms clean and fully stocked with supplies? Were all toilets, sinks, and hand dryers working?

Name _____ Class _____ Date _____

Chapter  14 Study Guide   Risk Management

Part 1   True or False

Directions   Indicate whether each statement is true or false by placing a check mark in the column at the right.

		True	*False*
1.	The possibility of incurring a loss is a risk.	_____	_____
2.	Insurance is a common form of protection against risk.	_____	_____
3.	The amount the policyholder pays for insurance coverage is the claim.	_____	_____
4.	An independent insurance agent sells policies written by only one company.	_____	_____
5.	Workers' compensation is insurance that pays employees injured on the job.	_____	_____
6.	A copyright is a name or symbol that identifies a company's product.	_____	_____

Part 2   Completion

Directions   In the Answers column, write the word or words needed to complete each sentence.

Answers

7. A(n) (?) can result in personal losses such as health and well-being.   _____

8. Risk that relates to harm or injury to others or their property is (?).   _____

9. A(n) (?) agrees to take on risks and pay for losses if they occur.   _____

10. (?) includes software, music, books, and movies.   _____

11. The person or company buying an insurance policy is the (?).   _____

12. (?) refers to illegal uses of patents, trademarks, and copyrights.   _____

Part 3   Types of Risk

Directions   In the Answers column, indicate which type of risk is described by each statement.

A. economic risk   C. pure risk   E. controllable risk   G. insurable risk
B. non-economic risk   D. speculative risk   F. uncontrollable risk   H. uninsurable risk   *Answers*

13. This risk is not common, and the amount of loss is impossible to predict.   13. _____

14. You cannot reduce the risk by actions you take.   14. _____

15. The three categories include personal risk, property risk, and liability risk.   15. _____

16. You can reduce or eliminate the loss by actions you take.   16. _____

17. You may be inconvenienced, but you will not incur financial impact.   17. _____

18. A tornado, blizzard, or flood is an example of this type of risk.   18. _____

19. Many people face the risk, and the cost of possible losses can be predicted.   19. _____

20. This risk offers the chance either to gain or to lose.   20. _____

Part 4 Activities

21. An insurance agent represents an insurance company and sells policies to individuals and businesses. Insurance agents may work for one large insurance company and sell only the policies written by that company, or they may be independent agents that sell many types of policies from a number of different companies. Contact two insurance agents in your community—one who works for only one large insurance company and another who is an independent agent. Interview both agents to find out about the policies they offer and the companies they represent. What are the advantages and disadvantages of purchasing insurance from an agent who represents just one large insurance company? What are the advantages and disadvantages of purchasing insurance from an independent agent who represents many different companies? After you have interviewed both agents, prepare a report of your findings.

22. Companies purchase insurance to protect their business in three main areas—personnel, property, and operations. Review the types of risks involved in each of the three areas. Then prepare a visual representation, such as a poster or a PowerPoint presentation, illustrating the various kinds of damage or loss that a business might sustain in each of the categories and the types of policies that companies could purchase to protect themselves against such damage or loss.

23. Most businesses offer their employees insurance as part of their employee benefits package. The cost of the insurance may be paid in full by the employer or may be shared by the employer and employee. Types of insurance offered can include health insurance, which may cover medical expenses, hospitalizations, and prescription drugs. Some companies also may offer optional insurance for dental or vision expenses. Other types of insurance may include life insurance and disability insurance. Contact the employee benefits department at several large companies in your community and ask about the insurance benefits that are offered to employees. What percentage of the premiums is paid by the employer and by the employee? What is the estimated value of the insurance benefits over and above the employee's salary? Prepare a chart that compares the benefits offered by each of the companies that you contacted. Do you think that a company that offers an attractive insurance benefits package may have a competitive edge when recruiting new employees?

Chapter  15 Study Guide   Consumers in the Global Economy

Part 1   Agree or Disagree

Directions   Indicate whether you agree or disagree with each of the following
statements by placing a check mark in the column at the right.

		Agree	Disagree
1.	AHAM develops performance standards for appliances, such as refrigerators.	_____	_____
2.	A good source for recommendations of products is the Better Business Bureau.	_____	_____
3.	The unit price for a 12-ounce box of cereal that costs $2.39 is 20 cents an ounce.	_____	_____
4.	A clearance sale is used to clear goods that the store no longer wishes to carry.	_____	_____
5.	Private label brands are sold only to members of private shopping clubs.	_____	_____
6.	Products sold at factory outlets sometimes contain minor flaws.	_____	_____
7.	Small claims courts prohibit the use of lawyers and witnesses.	_____	_____
8.	When a business controls the market for a product, it has a monopoly.	_____	_____

Part 2   Matching

Directions   In the Answers column, write the letter that represents the word, or
group of words, that correctly matches each statement.

				Answers
9.	The use of a third party to resolve a complaint	A. impulse buying	9.	_____
10.	Providing false information to consumers to make a sale	B. express warranty	10.	_____
11.	A name given to a product to distinguish it from similar items	C. arbitration	11.	_____
12.	An unstated warranty imposed by law and understood to apply	D. fraud	12.	_____
13.	Results in a decision that is legally binding	E. implied warranty	13.	_____
14.	A promise of a quality of performance made orally or in writing	F. mediation	14.	_____
15.	Buying too quickly, often at or near the checkout counter	G. brand	15.	_____

Part 3   Government Agencies

Directions   In the Answers column, write the initials of the government agency that would be
most concerned with the following consumer problems.

		Answers
16.	A skin care product that causes a serious rash	_____
17.	A company that is using unfair business practices to eliminate competition	_____
18.	A lesser quality of beef that is advertised as "prime"	_____
19.	An infant seat with a handle that does not latch properly	_____
20.	A power plant releasing unsafe emissions into the air	_____

Part 4 Activities

21. Many products are so widely advertised that we immediately associate the brand name with the product. Column 1 lists categories of products. In Column 2, write the first brand name that comes to mind for each product.

COLUMN 1   **COLUMN 2**

1. Facial tissues   1. _____

2. Photocopier   2. _____

3. Transparent tape   3. _____

4. Cola drink   4. _____

5. Flavored gelatin   5. _____

22. The word "sale" is used prominently in many advertisements to attract customers to a particular business, product, or service. From past issues of your local newspaper or brochures/flyers that you may receive in the mail, cut out six ads that prominently feature the word "sale." Attach each ad to a separate piece of paper. Below each ad, indicate whether the sale being advertised is a promotional sale or a clearance sale. For each ad, point out how effective you think the ad is at attracting customers. Explain your answer.

23. Consumers may obtain product information in several ways. Often the brand name itself provides consumers with information about the product. Product labels often describe the contents or special characteristics of the product. Seals of approval provide consumers with assurances of quality. The first column below lists product information that could be found in a product name, on a label, or on a seal. For each item listed, place a check mark in the appropriate column to indicate whether the information would be found in a product name, on a label, or on a seal.

Product Information	Product Name	Label	Seal
1. Recommended by *Good Housekeeping*	_____	_____	_____
2. Dry clean only	_____	_____	_____
3. Brand of computer	_____	_____	_____
4. 50% cotton and 50% polyester	_____	_____	_____
5. Model of automobile	_____	_____	_____
6. UL tested and approved	_____	_____	_____
7. Brand of breakfast cereal	_____	_____	_____
8. Hand wash in cold water, lay flat to dry	_____	_____	_____
9. Approved by Motorist Assurance Program	_____	_____	_____
10. Size L (large)	_____	_____	_____

Name _____ Class _____ Date _____

Chapter  17 Study Guide Banking and Financial Services

Part 1 True or False

Directions Decide whether each of the following statements is true or false. If the statement is true, write *true* in the Answers column. If the statement is false, write the term in the Answers column that will make the statement true.

Answers

1. The **Federal Reserve System (Fed)** supervises and regulates member banks.   1. _____
2. A fee a bank charges for handling a checking account is a **penalty**.   2. _____
3. A **credit card** is used for ATM transactions.   3. _____
4. A **cease-and-desist order** is written notice to the bank not to pay a check.   4. _____
5. **Electronic funds transfer** uses technology for banking activities.   5. _____
6. A **certified check** is a check that a bank draws on its own funds.   6. _____
7. Banks offer **safe-deposit boxes** for the storage of valuables.   7. _____
8. An **endorsement** is written evidence that you received payment.   8. _____

Part 2 Completion

Directions In the Answers column, write the word or words needed to complete each sentence.

Answers

9. (?) make loans based on the value of some tangible object, such as jewelry.   9. _____
10. Prepaid cards for items such as phone service are called (?).   10. _____
11. When two or more people have a bank account together, it is called a (?).   11. _____
12. A(n) (?) is a separate book used for recording checking account activity.   12. _____
13. Special forms for making payments when you are away from home are (?).   13. _____

Part 3 Multiple Choice

Directions In the Answers column indicate which type of deposit institution is best described by each statement.

A. commercial banks
B. savings and loan associations
C. mutual savings banks
D. credit unions

Answers

14. Frequently have branch offices in shopping centers and grocery stores   14. _____
15. Accept savings deposits and make loans to members only   15. _____
16. Profits are distributed in proportion to the amount of business each participant does   16. _____
17. Often described as full-service banks because they offer a wide range of services   17. _____
18. Traditionally specialized in savings accounts and loans for home mortgages   18. _____

Activities and Study Guide – Student Edition

Part 4 Activities

19. Banks and other financial institutions are constantly competing for business, so from time to time they may offer special rates or services in order to attract new customers. Investigate several financial institutions in your community to learn more about the products and services they offer. What special rates or services, if any, are they currently offering? Are the special offers for new customers only? Are they for a specified period of time? After you have completed your research, prepare a visual representation, such as a chart, poster, or computer presentation, of your findings that highlights the products and services available from each financial institution you investigated. You also may want to include information on customer-friendly features, such as convenient locations and extended hours, which may attract new customers.

20. You have learned in this chapter about the three primary types of endorsement—blank endorsement, full endorsement (also called special endorsement), and restrictive endorsement. For each of the situations below, indicate how you would properly endorse the check.

Situation	Endorsement
1. Maria Alvarez has received a paycheck for $250, which she wishes to cash at her bank. She will need to use a blank endorsement on the check. Write the proper endorsement in the space at the right.	_____ _____ _____
2. Eric Myers has received a check for $385. Eric wants to endorse the check over to his brother, Jeff Myers, as partial payment on a personal loan. Write the proper full or special endorsement.	_____ _____ _____
3. Bookstore owner, Sandra Walker, has a personal check from one of her customers, payable to The Book Nook. Sandra wants to deposit the check into the store's account. Use a restrictive endorsement.	_____ _____ _____
4. Kristy Keller has received a check for $78 that she wishes to deposit into her savings account. The check, however, is made payable to Kristi Keller. Use the proper blank endorsement.	_____ _____

21. Stored-value cards are becoming increasingly popular. These prepaid cards have many convenient uses, such as paying for telephone services, highway tolls, and school lunches. Survey a group of your friends to discover the types of products or services for which they use stored-value cards. What do they consider the advantages of using these prepaid cards? Are there disadvantages? If so, what are they? Present the results of your survey in a brief report.

Name _____ Class _____ Date _____

Chapter ⬤18 Study Guide Consumer Credit

Part 1 Agree or Disagree

Directions Indicate whether you agree or disagree with each of the following
statements by placing a check mark in the column at the right.

Answers

	Agree	Disagree
1. A down payment is a partial payment made at the time of the purchase.	_____	_____
2. The date on which a loan must be repaid is known as the final payment date.	_____	_____
3. The three Cs of credit are character, capacity, and creditworthiness.	_____	_____
4. A credit bureau gathers and reports information on credit users.	_____	_____
5. Property that is used as security for a loan is called collateral.	_____	_____
6. The legal process of reducing or eliminating money owed is bankruptcy.	_____	_____
7. The annual percentage rate states the percentage cost of credit per month.	_____	_____
8. A credit counselor is employed by a collection agency.	_____	_____

Part 2 Unscramble

Directions Unscramble the following vocabulary words that were discussed in Chapter 18.

Answers

9. topsimnoyresor (2 words) _____

10. genrocis _____

11. decrit _____

12. cupnabyktr _____

13. trocalleal _____

Part 3 Matching

Directions In the Answers column, indicate which law is best described by each of
the statements below.

Answers

A. Truth-in-Lending Law of 1968   D. Fair Credit Reporting Act
B. Equal Credit Opportunity Act   E. Consumer Credit Reporting Reform Act
C. Fair Credit Billing Act   F. Fair Debt Collections Act

14. Allows you to withhold payment due on defective merchandise purchased with a credit card   14. ____

15. Places the burden of proof for accurate credit information on the credit reporting agency   15. ____

16. Requires lenders to clearly state the annual percentage rate and total finance charge   16. ____

17. Requires that debt collectors treat you fairly and bans certain debt collection actions   17. ____

18. Prohibits creditors from denying credit based on age, race, sex, or marital status   18. ____

19. Gives consumers the right to know what information credit bureaus are providing about them   19. ____

20. Protects consumers against unauthorized use of credit cards   20. ____

Part 4 Activities

21. Some information typically requested on credit applications is listed below. Place a check mark in the column at the right to indicate which of the three Cs is most closely related to each item.

Credit Application Information	Character	Capacity	Capital
1. Your employment history	_____	_____	_____
2. Your current salary	_____	_____	_____
3. The amount of debt you have	_____	_____	_____
4. The amount of money you have in savings	_____	_____	_____
5. Your credit record (how you pay your bills)	_____	_____	_____
6. Your checking account balance	_____	_____	_____
7. Your ability to pay your bills on time	_____	_____	_____
8. The value of your home (equity)	_____	_____	_____
9. Your reputation for honesty	_____	_____	_____
10. The value of other assets you own	_____	_____	_____

22. It is important to know what information is on your credit report because this can affect your ability to obtain additional credit. The Fair and Accurate Credit Transactions (FACT) Act of 2003 entitles consumers to obtain a free copy of their credit report each year from each of the three major credit reporting agencies—Experian, Equifax, and TransUnion. This will allow consumers to check their credit report for any unauthorized activity, including activity that may be the result of identity theft. Visit the website at http://www.annualcreditreport.com and review your free personal credit report. Did you find any errors on the report that could damage your credit rating or prevent you from obtaining credit? If so, you should take the appropriate steps to have the erroneous information removed from your credit report.

23. Sometimes the use of credit is appropriate, but other times it is not. Review each of the situations below and decide whether or not credit should be used. Indicate your answer by placing a check mark in the appropriate column at the right.

	Use of Credit?	
Situation	Yes	No
1. Andy has comparison shopped and found a lawnmower at an excellent sale price.	_____	_____
2. Julie sees a dress she wants. The price is high, and she doesn't have the cash.	_____	_____
3. Jim wants a new tennis racket. He sees a sign that says, "Buy now, and pay later."	_____	_____
4. Maggie wants to buy computer equipment to start a graphic design business.	_____	_____
5. Juan finds a good buy on furniture he needs for his home. The sale ends today.	_____	_____

Activities and Study Guide – Student Edition

Chapter  19 Study Guide   Savings and Investment Strategies

Part 1   True or False

Directions   Place a *T* for True or an *F* for False in the Answers column to show
whether each of the following statements is true or false.

Answers

1. Saving money in a systematic way is the basis for achieving your financial goals.   1. T
2. Investing in commodities is considered to be a very safe, stable alternative investment.   2. ____
3. Common stock represents ownership in a corporation and has priority over preferred stock.   3. F
4. A full-service broker provides information about securities you may want to purchase.   4. F
5. Many people buy municipal bonds because they are exempt from federal and most state taxes.   5. T
6. Series EE bonds are bought at full face value and pay a fixed rate of interest.   6. T
7. Monthly payments for adjustable-rate mortgages are often higher than fixed-rate mortgages.   7. F
8. Rare stamps, coins, art, and antiques are items on which investors can make a large profit.   8. T

Part 2   Matching

Directions   In the Answers column, write the letter that represents the word, or
group of words, that correctly matches the statement.

Answers

9. An investment fund that receives money from many investors.   A. yield   9. E
10. A business organization for the buying and selling of securities   B. liquidity   10. D
11. The annual percentage of money earned on savings or investments   C. market value   11. A
12. Items of personal interest to collectors that can increase in value   D. stock exchange   12. F
13. The ease with which an investment can be changed into cash   E. mutual fund   13. B
14. The price at which a share of stock can be bought or sold   F. collectibles   14. C

Part 3   Saving and Investment Choices

Directions   Identify the type of savings and investment choice being described by each of the
statements by placing a check mark in the correct column.

	Savings Account	Certificate of Deposit	Money Market	Stocks	Bonds
15. Lending money to businesses or governments					✓
16. Becoming part owner of a company				✓	
17. Penalties assessed for early withdrawal					✓
18. Deposit or withdraw money as needed	✓				
19. Must leave on deposit for a specified period		✓			
20. Variable interest rates based on government and corporate securities			✓		

Part 4 Activities

21. Some of the safest investments that you can make are those guaranteed by the U.S. government. Visit the website for the U.S. Department of the Treasury, Bureau of the Fiscal Service (https://www.fiscal.treasury.gov/) and review information about the different types of U.S. savings bonds, Treasury bills, and Treasury notes. Create a chart comparing each of these investment products. Indicate the minimum amount of money needed to purchase each item, the amount of time each must be held before it can be redeemed, and any other information that would help an investor decide which type of product to purchase.

22. Many people purchase real estate as an investment. They may keep the property to provide a monthly rental income or sell it for a profit as the value of the property increases. Talk to someone in your community who is a real estate investor. Why did he or she choose real estate as an investment? How many properties are owned? How are the properties being used? What are the advantages of investing in real estate? What are the disadvantages? After you have completed your interview, prepare a brief report of your findings. *they thought it was a market that would always be needed*

5, 2 rented out 3 unused   advantages are consistent, usual appreciation

23. In this chapter, you have learned about a number of ways to invest money in savings. For each of the *disadvantage* situations below, decide which type of savings plan would be most appropriate. Write the letter in the *is* Answers column. *liquidity*

    A. regular savings account

    B. money market account

    C. certificate of deposit

    D. mutual fund

Answers

1. Brittany wants to invest in stocks, but she wants to reduce her amount of risk.   *D*

2. Jesse wants his savings to earn money based on changes in current interest rates.   *B*

3. Natalie wants to save a small amount of money each week for a summer trip.   *C*

4. Azra wants to earn a higher rate of interest but wants easy access to her money.   *A*

5. Steve is willing to invest for a set time period in order to earn a higher interest rate.   *C*

6. Janie has $50 in birthday money that she wants to use to open a savings account.   *A*

7. Trevor has $2,500 that he wants to invest for four years to save for college.   *C*

Activities and Study Guide – Student Edition

Name _____ Class _____ Date _____

Chapter 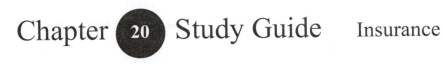 20 Study Guide Insurance

Part 1 Yes or No

Directions Indicate your answer to each of the following questions by placing a
check mark on the line under *yes* or *no* at the right.

	Yes	No
1. Do most states require drivers to carry automobile insurance?	_____	_____
2. Does property insurance cover damage to your home from natural disasters?	_____	_____
3. Does replacement insurance depreciate the value of personal property?	_____	_____
4. Does major medical insurance cover doctor's office visits?	_____	_____
5. Does your age affect the cost of your automobile insurance?	_____	_____
6. Does a renters' policy protect the actual dwelling?	_____	_____
7. Is insurance available to cover dental expenses and vision care?	_____	_____
8. Are most managed care plans run by state governments?	_____	_____

Part 2 Short Answer

Directions In the Answers column, write the word or words that best describes
each statement below.

Answers

9. An amount that you must pay before the insurance company pays a claim _____

10. The most common form of home and property insurance sold today _____

11. The person named to receive the benefits in a life insurance policy _____

12. Alternative health insurance plans, such as HMOs and PPOs _____

13. Provides daily assistance needed due to a lengthy illness or disability _____

14. Sharing of medical expenses by the policyholder and insurance company _____

Part 3 Types of Life Insurance

Directions Identify the type of life insurance being described by each of the statements by
placing a check mark in the correct column.

	Term Life	Permanent Life	Group Life
15. Has cash value and an investment feature	_____	_____	_____
16. Has no savings or investment features	_____	_____	_____
17. Offered through employers or organizations	_____	_____	_____
18. The least expensive form of life insurance	_____	_____	_____
19. Encourages people to save for the future	_____	_____	_____
20. Many people act together to buy insurance	_____	_____	_____
21. Includes whole life, variable life, and universal life insurance plans	_____	_____	_____

Part 4 Activities

22. As you have learned, companies that offer automobile insurance use certain factors to determine the cost of coverage. Those factors may include your age and academic standing, as well as other things. Contact several insurance companies in your community that offer vehicle insurance and obtain a quote for coverage. Provide each company with the same information about the vehicle and driver. Be sure to ask each company about any discounts they may offer, such as "good student" discounts, or reduced rates for participating in a driver's education program. After you have completed your research, create a chart or spreadsheet that compares the rates and discounts offered by each of the companies.

23. For each of the following situations, indicate the kind of health insurance that would best meet the needs.

1. Stan Matthews works at a home center store. While stocking painting supplies, he slipped and fell off a ladder, breaking his arm. What type of insurance would pay for Stan's medical expenses?

   _____

2. Sharon Henderson wants to have a choice of her medical providers, but she also wants to receive treatment at a discount. What type of plan should she choose?

   _____

3. While eating popcorn at the movies, Josh Palmer cracked a tooth. What kind of insurance will pay for the restorative dental work that Josh will need?

   _____

4. Wendy Swanson wants to pay a fixed monthly fee and have a wide range of health care services provided to her by a staffed medical clinic. What kind of plan should she select?

   _____

5. Charlene Redman had to have her appendix removed. What type of insurance would be needed to cover the surgeon's fee for the operation?

   _____

6. Paula Reese visits her eye doctor each year for an eye examination and purchases new glasses every two years. What type of insurance would help pay for some of these costs?

   _____

7. Doug Lightner wants a health insurance policy that covers hospital, surgical, regular medical, and major medical bills. What kind of policy should he select?

   _____

8. Rodney Shanahan was admitted to the hospital with severe stomach pains and was there for three days before being discharged. What kind of insurance would pay for most or all of Rodney's care while in the hospital?

   _____

DECISIONS, DECISIONS, DECISIONS—PART 2

A Decision-Making Project

As a consumer, worker, and citizen, you constantly make decisions that affect your future—both personally and financially. Some of these decisions are made quickly. Others require time, research, and careful deliberation.

In this project, you will make various personal and business decisions, based on your personal goals, values, and business knowledge. Each situation you will consider presents several choices you can make, but each choice will have financial consequences. Therefore, you should choose carefully. Random events that are based on chance also will affect you financially. The components of this project are:

DECISIONS: For each decision, you will have three alternatives from which to choose. You should consider not only the immediate effects of your decision but also how it will affect your future.

CONSEQUENCES: These are direct results of the decisions you will be making. Your teacher will provide you with the consequences as they are needed.

RANDOM EVENTS: Random events are beyond your control. However, they still affect your financial situation. Cut out the numbered slips of paper below and place them in a bag or box. When instructed to do so, you will draw a number that will indicate how you will be affected by the random event.

After you have made your decision for each situation, you will record the financial result on the summary sheet at the end of the project. Each decision, consequence, or random event will either increase or decrease your balance. At the end of the project, calculate your final balance.

Your teacher will assign you to work individually or in a group. If you are assigned to work in a group, you should discuss your decisions with other group members and arrive at a shared decision.

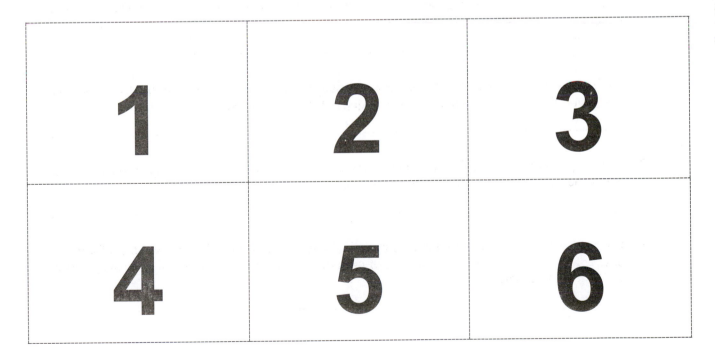

Procedures

1. Review the decision-making steps in Chapter 1 of the textbook.
2. Encourage students to consider all factors affecting their decisions rather than making selections based on the immediate payoff.
3. Assign students to work individually or in teams.
4. Remind students that after each situation they must record an increase or decrease on the summary sheet.

Instructional Approach

Students can be assigned to work individually or as part of a team. Each team may consist of two to four members. If students are assigned to work in teams, they must discuss each decision and form a team decision. If a team approach is used, each team should use only one summary sheet.

Additional Suggestions

- Require students to conduct outside research before making some of the decisions.
- Ask students to discuss their decisions with parents or others before they make them.
- Review business terms and concepts to make sure students have a clear understanding.
- Discuss career opportunities related to some of the situations in the project.
- Use student helpers to provide results of consequences to individuals or groups.
- If available, dice present a more streamlined method of generating random numbers one through six than do slips of paper.

Required Time

The time needed for this project can vary from one to four class sessions depending on the length of the class period and the time used for discussion. Time will be needed to introduce students to the format and procedures of the project. In addition, follow-up questions are provided for post-simulation discussion.

Evaluation Techniques

Because correct answers vary, a grade of "complete" or "incomplete" is probably most appropriate. In addition, students can be evaluated based on math accuracy, class discussion of situations, and interpersonal relations when working with other students.

To help students evaluate their own performance, pose some of the follow-up questions. You may also wish to ask students if they were able to follow the decision-making process outlined in Chapter 1. Were their decisions overly influenced by the monetary payoff? If they worked in groups, did all group members participate in the decisions? Through such questioning, you will enable students to see that there is a methodical way of approaching decision making, despite the many, sometimes unknown, factors affecting their decisions.

Activities and Study Guide – Student Edition

Situation 1—Decision—Family Status

You must determine your family situation. With each choice, you start with $6,000 in savings, but remember that future Decisions and Consequences will be affected by this Decision. Record the $6,000 on your summary sheet.

Choice A	Choice B	Choice C
single, sharing an apartment with another person	married, no children	married, one two-year-old child

Situation 2—Decision—Using Credit

You want to borrow money to buy a two-year-old car. Decide where you want to obtain a loan and record the amount of the down payment on your summary sheet.

Choice A	Choice B	Choice C
obtain a loan from the bank with a required down payment of	obtain a loan from your credit union with a required down payment of	obtain a loan from a consumer finance company with a required down payment of

Situation 3—Decision—Automobile Insurance

You need automobile insurance and have the following choices. Select the type of coverage you desire and record the amount on your summary sheet. You may want to investigate each option carefully before making your decision.

Choice A	Choice B	Choice C
full coverage, no deductible	full coverage with $100 deductible for damage to your car	bodily injury and property damage liability coverage only (no coverage for your car)

Situation 4—Random Event—Inflation/Deflation

Recent economic conditions have affected consumer prices. Select a number to determine how you will be affected. Record the result on your summary sheet.

Result 1 low inflation	Result 2 moderate inflation	Result 3 no inflation	Result 4 slight deflation	Result 5 high inflation	Result 6 low inflation

Situation 5—Consequence—Family Expenses

As a result of your decision in Situation 1, you have encountered additional living expenses. Obtain the amount to be recorded on your summary sheet from your teacher.

Situation 6—Decision—Financial Records

In order to keep accurate personal financial records, select one of the following record-keeping methods. Record the amount on your summary sheet.

Choice A	Choice B	Choice C
use your checkbook as your spending and budget record	purchase a multicolumn record book	purchase a personal budget/home financial planning computer program

Situation 7—Random Event—Increased/Decreased Savings

Select a number to determine which of the following events will influence your financial situation. Record the amount on your summary sheet.

Result 1	Result 2	Result 3	Result 4	Result 5	Result 6
unexpected medical expenses	unexpected tax refund	additional amount owed for taxes	unexpected salary bonus	unexpected tax refund	additional amount owed for taxes

Situation 8—Decision—Health Insurance

Your employer provides health and medical insurance coverage that covers only certain situations. You must decide if you wish to add additional insurance.

Choice A	Choice B	Choice C
additional health insurance to cover 90 percent of all medical expenses	full coverage for all medical and hospital expenses	no additional health insurance

Situation 9—Random Event—Your Credit Rating

Various circumstances have affected your credit costs. Select a number to determine how you are affected. Record the amount on your summary sheet.

Result 1	Result 2	Result 3	Result 4	Result 5	Result 6
early payments (lower finance charge)	one late payment (penalty)	early payments	early payments	early payments	late payments

Situation 10—Consequence—Auto Accident

As a result of a recent auto accident, your car has been damaged. See your teacher for the repair costs, which will be based on your decision about automobile insurance in Situation 3. Be sure to record the amount on your summary sheet.

Situation 11—Random Event—Salary Bonus

Based on your job performance, you have earned a salary bonus. Select a number to determine the amount. Record the amount on your summary sheet.

Result 1	Result 2	Result 3	Result 4	Result 5	Result 6

Situation 12—Decision—Investment Choice

You wish to invest part of your savings. Select one of the following investment plans. Record your choice on your summary sheet.

Choice A	Choice B	Choice C
purchase stocks with current market value of $300 plus broker commission	invest $300 in mutual fund with no commission fee	place $300 in savings certificate at local financial institution

Situation 13—Random Event—Insurance Rates

Your driving record has affected your automobile insurance rates. Select a number to determine the effect. Record the amount on your summary sheet.

Result 1	Result 2	Result 3	Result 4	Result 5	Result 6
good driving record	several accidents	good driving record	speeding ticket	completed driver's education	good driving record

Situation 14—Consequence—Medical Expenses

You have received a number of unexpected hospital and doctor bills. See your teacher for the amount you must pay as a result of the decision you made in Situation 8. Be sure to record the amount on your summary sheet.

Situation 15—Random Event—Investment Return

Based on your past investments, you have earned dividends and interest. Select a number to determine the amount. Record the results on your summary sheet.

Result 1	Result 2	Result 3	Result 4	Result 5	Result 6

Situation 16—Consequence—Budget Problems

You have just examined your financial records. See your teacher for the results of the record keeping system you chose in Situation 6. Record the amount on your summary sheet.

Situation 17—Consequence—Investment Return

See your teacher for the result of your investment decision in Situation 12.

Name _____ Class _____ Date _____

DECISIONS, DECISIONS, DECISIONS—PART 2—SUMMARY SHEET

	SITUATION	TOPIC	CHOICE	AMOUNT	BALANCE
1.	Decision	Family Status	A	+ 6,000	6,000
2.	Decision	Using Credit	A	– 900	5,100
3.	Decision	Automobile Insurance	A	– 350	4,750
4.	Random Event	Inflation/Deflation	3	+/– 0	4750
5.	Consequence	Family Expenses		–275	4475
6.	Decision	Financial Records	C	– 65	4410
7.	Random Event	Increased/Decreased Savings	1	+/– 40	4370
8.	Decision	Health Insurance	B	– 350	4020
9.	Random Event	Your Credit Rating	2	+/– 20	4000
10.	Consequence	Auto Accident		– 0	4000
11.	Random Event	Salary Bonus	5	+ 850	4850
12.	Decision	Investment Choice	B	– 300	4550
13.	Random Event	Insurance Rates	1	+/– 40	4590
14.	Consequence	Medical Expenses		– 0	4590
15.	Random Event	Investment Return	4	+ 200	4790
16.	Consequence	Budget Problems		– 0	4790
17.	Consequence	Investment Return		+/– 340	5130
				FINAL BALANCE	5130

Student Comments

1. Which decisions might you have made differently? Why?

2. What factors did you forget to consider when making a decision?

3. What advice would you give to someone about making financial decisions?

Activities and Study Guide – Student Edition